AN AMARANTHINE SUMMER

EDITED AND INTRODUCED BY
SHANE WARREN and RYAN WASSER

Cover design by Shay Culligan

ISBN 978-1-954353-19-0

Kelsay Books.com
501 S 1040 E
A119
American Fork, Utah 84003

For Kim Bridgford

Deyr fé,

deyja frændr,

deyr sjálfr it sama.

En orðstírr

deyr aldregi

hveim er sér góðan getr.

* * *

Cows die,

family die,

you will die the same way.

But a good reputation

never dies

for one who earns it well.

—Havamal 76

CONTENTS

FOREWORD by Ryan Wasser

I remember the evening drives from Coatesville to West Chester during my first semester back at university. The nights were, as one might expect of a mid-winter class, already dark by the time I departed my East Fallowfield driveway, but there was a brightness to them; the muted resplendence of post-Yule flurries helps to maintain that unspoken magical quality that usually dies out by the second or third week of January. That crispness makes you feel alive even if it compels you toward feeling as if you should go back inside and find something less chilly to do. Hot chocolate is apropos under such circumstances. But, for the first time since my release from the Army, I had somewhere important to be. And so, every Wednesday night, around six-thirty or so, I fell into my old, ramshackle Mustang and sped down Route 162 toward campus.

Anybody who has spent any amount of time at West Chester University will understand what I mean when I say that Main Hall has a certain peculiar comfort to it, even if that comfort comes in the form of rooms without adequate temperature control, windows that don't open all the way (exacerbating the previous issue), and the less-than-fully-stocked vending machines with unreasonably priced foodstuffs purchased by students whose eating habits some might consider "questionable" in the best of cases. Main Hall is comfortable in the way an old house is comfortable—the mugginess of its interior beckons you in like your grandma, all smelling of coffee and nicotine; whose sole purpose in life you was to hug you at the waist because she was a foot shorter than you, and to sneak twenty dollars into your back pocket when your parents weren't looking. It always felt as if the professoriate of the English department—each in his or her own way—embodied some aspect of this parental caring for its students. Some, such as my friend and mentor, Dr. Paul Maltby, were (and are) classically trained lecturers, whose orderliness and precision bely a staunch paternalistic concern laser-focused on developing the sharpest minds possible. Others, such as Luanne Smith, cultivated creativity in her students through what can only be described as unbridled warmth and kindness, which, it should be noted, is never to be conflated with "easiness."

Dr. Kim Bridgford—Kim for those who knew her—was an entirely different kind of professor: I don't remember precisely what she was wearing the night I met her, but I do remember her debouching into our upper-level poetry seminar with a purposefulness that I hadn't noticed in other educators until that point. Dr. Bridgford was slender, a bit on the shorter side with dark hair, a soft, evenly-toned voice, and a penchant for animal print coats and fancy flats. Scarves may have been involved occasionally, but even if they weren't, for some reason, I can still picture one trailing behind her as she triumphantly assumed control of the room. She was one part "tiny troubadour" (to borrow from one of our authors, Leslie Schulz), and one part drill sergeant: I used to joke that Dr. Bridgford liked to handle her students with kid gloves; it just so happened that those gloves were cast iron and riveted. Still, within that toughness resonated an undeniable authenticity that I believe even the most cynical student was forced to respect.

I won't mince words: Dr. Bridgford demanded a lot of her students—an imposing proposition for a guy just returning to school for the first time in nearly a decade—and that demand was legitimized by the impressive oeuvre that we all knew she was responsible for, but hardly ever talked about. Animal print and imaginary scarves aside, Dr. Bridgford was always modest, at least as long as I knew her and especially as it pertained to her craft. While she was exceptionally skilled at freeform poetry, her real gift was the way she worked with form. One collection of sestinas—the name of which escapes me—was something of a legend for creative writing students at West Chester University because of the sheer amount of time it took to produce. The mere *idea* of it set a precedent for the kind of work that lay ahead of us. And her work with sonnets, the work she seemed most prolific at, is truly something to behold. Titles like *Undone*, *Instead of Maps*, and *In the Extreme: Sonnets about World Records* are all award-worthy or winning endeavors. That said, it's the singular poems like "Why Sisyphus Isn't a Woman" that stuck with me if only because of the playful and poignant antagonism they presented for somebody as invested in philosophy as I am. Yes, yes . . . Dr. Bridgford demanded the best of us, and her demands came by example; because of that, we willingly ground ourselves to dust in her workshop. And we were all the better for it.

Reflecting on time spent with an educator like Dr. Bridgford raises a pertinent if not hifalutin question for a person such as myself: what "is" a professor in the first place? Taken at its face, the notion is simple enough—hardly worth an in-depth discussion. But grasped at its root, the word references one who affirms and lays claim to knowledge openly. A professor *is* avowed to Truth, and the solemnity of such being-avowed is only matched in its profundity by the effect such professing has on others, regardless of their station or status within the hierarchies of culture and academia. Personal experience has taught me as much; I simply would not be the writer I am today had I not the opportunity to study with such a formidable individual. In an era where academia is content with current laissez-faire approaches to student expectations, Dr. Bridgford unapologetically called for "more" and hopefully received "more" in return, especially from me.

This anthology is a testament to that formidability. Included in the list of authors are former students, mentees of a strictly professional nature, acquaintances from both West Chester and Fairfield Universities where Dr. Bridgford taught, and individuals invested in Poetry by the Sea, the conference she established. The first part of the book, "Summertime Poems," is a wealth of material from published and unpublished poets alike—each poem disclosing a facet of slow, languid months long since passed. The second part of the book, "Summertime Stories," speaks to the different relationships of the summer: relationships with friends, with family, with the ocean, with possible lovers, and most of all with the year itself. I hope, dear reader, that you'll enjoy reading these works as much as I did while putting this anthology together.

I'd like to take a brief moment to mention my good friend and co-editor Shane Warren, who endured some serious medical crises this year. I won't go into the details of those events—it is not my place to do so in the first place—but I feel as though it should be known that this project was, by and large, *his* idea. Shane, for those who don't know him, is my inverted doppelganger: whereas I obtained my degrees in English before pursuing philosophy, Shane obtained his Masters in philosophy first and is currently in West Chester's creative writing program, which hopefully he'll return to finish in the near future. While I would not attempt to speak to his inner thoughts, I remember how he "was" during that first semester in the English program, casually strolling into our writing center as he always did, new poems rolled up in his hands like some mystical scroll; an excited glint in his eyes betrayed an exuberance that transcended his typically jovial self. I think I still have some of those poems in draft form. My good fortune to be able to work with such a creative spirit never ceases to amaze me, but I digress . . . for anybody who knows Shane Warren, his being of higher spirits than he normally was, speaks volumes about his engagement with Dr. Bridgford. As with me, she challenged him in the best of ways, and that meaningful challenge manifested itself in the way he carried himself day-to-day. I miss seeing my friend that excited and happy.

I think I could easily spend another four or five pages sharing memories of my interactions with Dr. Bridgford. Whether she was forbidding me to use questionable language, or indulging yet another visit from me during her office hours, or introducing me to the work of a poet who would become especially meaningful to me, she exerted an enormous influence on me as a writer and a person. To a lesser or greater extent—although most would be inclined to argue the "greater" extent—Dr. Bridgford held sway over each and every author involved in this anthology. She was a giant despite her physical stature, and she made each one of us better in ways we likely have yet to discover. One can only hope to live up to the towering example she set for us.

Ryan Wasser
MA, English Studies
West Chester University
December 2020

SUMMERTIME POEMS

Vince Carcirieri

Midway

In life we have two opportunities to become
a better son or daughter
when at the beach's Midway:
One: if you were too self-absorbed as a child before,
opt for two: win her the stuffed animal
when you're an adult.

Terese Coe

Puck, that Imp!

It's gift enough to fall in love
though lovers think they choose it;
the powers Puck most laughs to grant
are when and how to lose it.
When lovers are desperate, on the make
for misguided schemes to con the prize,
Puck will laugh at their tender ache—
the imp will do his worst!

Puck rules them all to accommodate
the love that can't be bidden,
can't be taken, tied, or brokered,
nor even mediocre—
Puck won't let you make love do
what he cannot allow it to.

Courage of a Poet

In little garrets slant and tight
alive with grave pursuings
the poets settle down to write
of each of their misdoings.

How brave they are. To persevere,
how daedal, how outlandish!
In motley on the rude frontier,
with whetted words to brandish.

However they eulogize the dead
or satirize Titania
or exalt their childhood quadruped,
it's seen as egomania.

Previously published in *Orchards Poetry Journal*

As Wild as We

Whose woods these are I think I know.
They call me from the village though,
and while I walk here, they are mine:
these willow, alder, elm and pine.

These maple, live oak, mountain ash,
chestnut, birch and sassafras,
the ponderosa, banyan, beech,
and sycamore, catalpa, peach.

The woods that grow as wild as we,
and spring like us, like us as free—
they call me from the village low,
and we can stay, or we can go.

And we can stay, or we can go.
Or lie among pistachio,
and laurel, larch or linden tree
and boxwood, lemon, ebony.

And drink the juice of tangerine,
and love on beds of frangipan,
and weave a wreath of cicely
with cherries from the cherry tree

and hazelnuts and holly bright
to match your hazel eyes tonight,
and never go where we are known
without the green we call our own.

Previously published in *Miller's Pond*

William Conelly

An Appreciation

She nudged green talents
from the shade of other poets.
Every novice knew:
inquire and she'd point up
the courses best for you.

Mulling how to fence
stampeding, raw experience
into a canny narrative?
She'd smile and short list
real alternatives;

yet managed well enough
not to manage stuff
too closely. She set folks
carving their own schemes
through spans of English oak.

Lending speech to spirit,
she helped us hear it
—the measured choices
folded into metaphor—
the range of mortal voices.

Barbara Crooker

Down the Shore

August arrives, round as a melon
bursting with juice,
carnival nights, the lights
dancing in water that
eddies around the pier, reflects the
fat moon's shimmies, a disco
globe revolving in a dark dance
hall, where waitresses and lifeguards
in cutoffs have come to
jitterbug, looking for a
kind of
love that summer
memories are made of,
nothing for a lifetime, just
one night, when everything's
perfect, your body firm as a peach, no
quarrels, no
running out of the car
slamming the door, just
this simmering night
under the boardwalk of stars,
velvet sand on bare feet,
waves kissing ankles, toes, tiny
x's marking the spot where
your lips finally meet, on the
zenith of summer, watermelon August.

Previously published in *Mezzo Cammin*

This American Life

where Annette, in Beach Blanket Bingo,
shook her brunette curls, called
to Frankie, batting her baby browns,
to come over and cover her in Coppertone.
Damn. That girl was hot. Doo-wop
on the portable radio, feet drumming
Land of 1000 Dances on the hot sand.
Fetch me my sunglasses, she cooed.
And go get me a coke and a hot dog,
pretty please. How about some Hostess
Ho-Ho's, too? July, and the sun
beating down upon the roof. Juicy
Fruit, Jujubes at the movies. Keep
the hits coming on KLUV, top forties
radio. Little Latin Lupe Lu. Then Maybelline.
Your mama said there'd be days like this.
Madras plaid shorts, perky headbands,
ponytails bouncing. Then quiet nights
under the stars, driftwood fires, sparks
rising. S'mores, their sticky sweetness
in the salty air. Throw more branches
on the fire. Very soon, Vietnam
will catch us in its undertow. War
with no exit plan. You're only nineteen.
Your chances of getting out are just
about none. But tonight, algorithms
be damned, the sun's going down
with a sizzle, and look, there's the moon,
bathing us all in its false zirconia,
its dreamy zaftig zero light.

Previously published in *Mezzo Cammin*

This Summer Day

That sprinkler is at it again,
hissing and spitting its arc
of silver, and the parched
lawn is tickled green. The air
hums with the busy traffic
of butterflies and bees,
who navigate without lane
markers, stop signs, directional
signals. One of my friends
says we're now in the shady
side of the garden, having moved
past pollination, fruition,
and all that bee-buzzed jazz,
into our autumn days. But I say wait.
It's still summer, and the breeze is full
of sweetness spilled from a million petals;
it wraps around your arms, lifts the hair
from the back of your neck.
The salvia, coreopsis, roses
have set the borders on fire,
and the peaches waiting to be picked
are heavy with juice. We are still ripening
into our bodies, still in the act of becoming.
Rejoice in the day's long sugar.
Praise that big fat tomato of a sun.

Previously published in *New Works Review*

Jeremiah Glass

Mourning Star

Stars do not end.
They are carried on,
in spirals,
in whorls,
in sparks
and arcs
and shades

that billow,
that tatter the dark,
that shape it,
own it,
bring it peace.

For the call
of the dark is secret,
and secrets
keep
the heart safe.

The stars though,
the stars,
they offer
arms to
pour secrets into,

yawning
into the darkness,
embracing it,
reaching
across the vastness eternal,

lightening the path
of eaten dreams,
warming strangled tongues
so they uncoil,
blazing golden memories
through the widowed heart.

What stars strike,
they stir:
profoundly;
subtly;
but always blessing it with verve.

The stars do not expire,
they transform:
everything.

Charlotte Innes

The Kestrel

A kestrel plunges from the sky,
whirling up a cloud of starlings
from a willow. They flare and pulse
in loose formation like a mass
of thoughts that aren't quite making sense,
till rain drives off the kestrel, and the starlings
dip and settle. I go inside,
marveling at the birds' communal
choreography, the way
they cleverly deflect invaders.
Our friends arrive with wine. We eat
grilled burgers with fresh bread and fruit.
Someone says that it's essential,
in the face of modern irony,
for art to illustrate compassion—
that people need to see *at least*
the possibility of peace.
In the light of two red candles,
my friends' faces glow and soften.
My dear friends. Here is peace
for just a moment. As night comes on,
we lie out on the deck and scan
the stars. A bat flits quickly round
the house, and then—no sound.
Chilled, we go inside for coffee,
and for more comfortable talk
on everything possessing us.

Previously published in *Descano Drive,* Kelsay Books, 2017

Pandemical #14

The village I cannot visit now slides
in glimpses through my thoughts, the cows grazing
meadows by the River Soar that lie
across from a field where my father's aging

into earth, his quiet body giving
way at last to what we're all made of.
I'm oddly shaken to think my body's a living
piece of him, so he's still here, laid

to rest, but living on in me. Cliché
you'd think, but having felt so separate for
so long (*My life! My life!*) I cannot say
what all this means to me, except that more

of me is *there* than I had thought. But oh,
I want to see the village, my stepmother's garden,
to hear the blackbird's song, to smell a rose,
clink *cheers* and talk of jaunts we might embark on.

Jean L. Kreiling

Jumping the Waves

Not strong swimmers,
not sailors,
not fishermen,
we were experts
at the kid stuff:

digging the holes
Mom said would lead to China;

walking to the jetty
half a mile down the beach;

collecting shells,
mostly broken;

and wading out to the spot where,
if we pushed off with our feet
at just the right moment,
we would rise up with a wave,
ascending into the sky,
becoming tall and buoyant and graceful
as the wave flowed through us,
then broke behind us
while we looked for the next one.
We called it jumping the waves.

But we were lifted more than we jumped;
we were carried
like seaweed,
rocked
like oversized newborns.
we floated
like foam,

our bodies fluid,
part of the salty, rolling wonder
that was our summer playground.

Dad had taken us out there when we were little,
holding us in his strong, hairy arms:
big sister first,
me two summers later,
then our little sister with the sun-kissed hair.
By the time he took our brother out,
my older sister and I had learned to do it on our own—
but she soon preferred sun-bathing.

I, on the other hand, never outgrew
my need for rocking.

Summer Evening
after the painting by Childe Hassam

One summer evening when the sun has barely
begun to sink, she contemplates the game
of clocks and customs, habits that unfairly
call this "evening," as if it were the same
as winter dusk. These burnished hours expose
what all her less considered hours have meant;
the lens has widened, just before its close,
to light both merciless and transient.
This golden sky fends off night's creeping gray
and renders her geraniums more red,
her dress more white, her almost-ended day
more like the first line of a still-unread,
perhaps unwritten, poem that might tell
the secrets of a summer day's farewell.

Twilight, Westhampton Beach

We who truly loved the ocean stayed—
not sated by our afternoon of sun,
not bored as waves repetitively played
with wind and light. The day was nearly done,
and still we stayed, our parents giving in
when we still craved the water and the sand,
addicted to the heartbeat-hailing din
of breakers' bluster teasing tender land.
The less enchanted left—they'd had their swim
and picnic lunch, they'd found their perfect shell;
they didn't watch the sinking sunlight skim
the water in its lingering farewell.
Our parents let us stay—and now I wonder
if they too felt the spell that we were under.

Previously published in *Coldnoon Travel Poetics*

Karen Kelsay

In a Hat Box

When I wake at three in the morning with stars
sprinkled between my curtains, and see
my old hatbox wedged on the corner shelf
beneath scalloped shadows, I remember

its contents of unused wool from a needlepoint
canvas, colored pencils, and the camera
with a broken lens. I recall a length of ribbon
too dark for my hair, business cards

that no longer matter, a plastic harmonica
from an amusement hall and an old monogrammed
handkerchief wrapped around a black and white
picture of you leaning against a palm tree.

Back then, you were a transplanted Nebraskan
collecting San Diego summers in your pockets,
exploring tide pools and sailboats. Each Saturday,
you rode the bus to Hotel Del Coronado

where big band music filled the Victorian ballroom.
One night you posed on the lawn in pearls and heels
beneath a sand dollar moon embedded above the bay.
That was before you married dad. Before trips

to Bermuda and Europe, mundane chores, diapers,
three children, bike rides, and sewing classes.
Before illness. When a slice of moon could move
across Coronado Bay and still glint in your eyes.

Jenna Le

Wheatfields

My mother's armoire
threw light like a star
on her cream-white duvet's
proud rose bouquets

as, legs crossed, she sat sifting
its hoard, by turns lifting
the jades and the pearls
and the gold chains aswirl

in their clamshell-like boxes,
the pendants and lockets.
Her sweater's wool itched,
mothball scent in each stitch,

when I leaned in to finger
a trinket. I'd linger
long on the splay
of her fragrant duvet,

feeling blessed to remain
in that special domain
beside her. Supine,
I tricked my own mind

into thinking each door
of her glossy armoire
was a lush field of wheat
spread under my feet,

a fairytale bounty.
There's no accounting,
but tonight, as we mounted
our honeymoon bed,

Dear, this memory fountained
back into my head…

Gillian Lynn Katz

Yesterday—Today and Tomorrow

"Yesterday, Today and Tomorrow"—
The name of the flower, purple and blue
in Johannesburg gardens of my youth.

Now that I'm grown those flowers are gone.
I'll never see that shade of blue
today, another day, or tomorrow.

So far away, the climate has changed
and now the flowers are a different hue
from the colorful gardens of my youth.

I never knew I'd travel so far
leave my homeland forever, no clue
yesterday, today or tomorrow.

My grandparents showed me those flowers
that sparkled in the morning dew
in Johannesburg gardens of my youth.

Now the gardens have changed,
there're different things I do.
In Scarsdale gardens
I have a new truth.

Elysian Fields

I want to be a buttercup
petals clustered
in a field of golden corolla,
tossing my head in a mass
of togetherness.

       I want to be one of the green leaves
       waving in the breeze
       laughing in the trees,
       a fertilized flower
       among the summer bees.

Not for me, the white-hooded
ladies of The Handmaid's Tale,
their shielded eyes
like blinders on a horse
staring straight ahead.

       I want to be the rain
       wet until eternity,
       dripping in company.

And in the center of Elysian Fields,
we can face the sun.

Retrospective

The trees I sit under are rain-drenched
leafy. I am two continents,
forty-five years away.
On my computer, an image—
A resplendent European Roller—
not one color missing on that bird;
Perched on a dried out tree twig
in the Kruger National Park
on the Facebook page
of a classmate
I'd long since forgotten.

Summer Study Abroad

The jumbo jet rolls down the runway,
you're aerodynamically transported away from me.
The ghost of your umbilical cord aches
inside. You take one more step
towards your sovereignty. I'll think
back to the time you were three,
when everything you did depended on me.

I'll dream of you floating in the Isle
of Capri. You swim like a nymph
in the waters of Compania.
You're rowed romantically on a gondola
in the city of Venezia. A proud mama bird
I let my fledgling fly free.
Exit the parking lot at LaGuardia
and pray for your safe journey on Alitalia.

Bruce McBirney

The Redwood Picnic Basket

I take it down and set it on a table;
a redwood picnic basket that my Dad
passed on with all the keepsakes that he had
from forebears. I look through them when I'm able—
young Jen (Grandma) on horseback at the stable
in, maybe, 1910; my great-granddad
just turned eighteen in Tandragee; a sad
obit; a diary; a family fable.
Much more than snapshots—vestiges of lives
that burned, and shook with frailty and laughter.
It's said, however stilled by what comes after,
old love remembered somehow still survives.
Dear parents, grandparents so long away,
I thought of you, and said your names today.

Richard Minot

A Summer Memory

Gosh Mommy,
can you buy me an ice cream cone?
'Cause I love chocolate
in the summer time
when it gets all drippy
going down my face,
and soon it's all gone
except for the cone.
C'est la vie honey,
c'est la vie.

Sally Nacker

Saying Goodbye

If my heart arrests, let it keep arresting.
I kept thinking of your willed words
as I walked one last time that spring
to your summerhouse. Birds

hopped and sang in the thickets on either side
of Veery Lane. The green
world trembled so bright I cried.
At the end of the long lane

the small, screened-in wood
house stood. Something fluttered inside it
like a large moth, or could
it be a bird, I thought

as I came closer. I saw then—
its nervous movement through the screen—
a little brown house wren.
I propped the door open between

the green world and the world inside,
stepped in, and drew
close to the frightened thing, tried
to guide it toward and through

the opening. I could tell
the wren's small heart was beating
wildly, could see its little eyes, so gentle.
Then off it flew into the trembling.

My Father's Eighty-Fifth Birthday

That day, I walked beside you, held
your cane, watched you push the mower

across the wide, May lawn. Thin, straight
lines were made, as in a poem.

The shorn grass flew back to the ground,
where it once grew; now cut from, yet

so at rest with, what it once knew.
Father, I loved the grass that day.

My New Gladness

Like the round bird and the rounded nest
the bird makes with the bird's breast—
           my new gladness.

Like the oval eggs the bird lays
in her round home where the bird stays—
           my sudden gladness.

The lightness of the roundness,
the birdsong against the soundless.

Chris O'Carroll

Top of the First

I will fling so fast, so crafty
that your strongest swing must fail.
The blow I wield, precise and mighty,
lets no throw of yours prevail.

Before the straining runner's gait,
the grass-stained dive, the dust-cloud slide,
our stances here define the contest—
wit vs. strength on either side.

Previously published in *Life and Legends*

July in Pennsylvania

The mockingbirds at Gettysburg prybar
their tails against the summer, lever at
some insubstantial weight. Between the stones
on which they perch, the memories of war
ride on the air as massive and as light
as breath elaborated into prayers
and slogans, platitudes and battle-cries.
Valor, glory, the cause, this hallowed ground—
these are the words the living heft and clang
above the voices of the birds. The dead
reply with wordless oratory. Breath
exhaled a long silence ago bears up
the outstretched wings as singers pause their songs
to swoop from monument to monument.

Previously published in *The Raintown Review*

Summer of the Shark

A seal population explosion
has sharks hunting close to this beach.
It's a hot day; I'd love to go swimming,
but I want to keep out of their reach.

News reports about fins in the surf
are enough to give anyone pause.
I'd rather my sun-and-sand selfies
did not look like outtakes from *Jaws*.

Though a dip would be cool and refreshing,
shark bites take forever to heal.
So I'm just wading up to my ankles,
trying hard not to look like a seal.

Previously published in *Light*

Julia Otto

Summer Vacations

As a wife to a partner
and a mom to a family,
we won't take many vacations
to Disney or a faraway beach getaway,
because instead
I'll buy a bright blue,
inflatable-3ft-deep—
warmed-by-nature's-heater—
smelling-of-chlorine-
and-plastic—
little-sanitizing-duck—
bobbing-"sunglasses-cool"—
kiddy-pool

for my average-sized yard
the kids'll stay cool
while I read in the sun;
human-wave-machine—
hand-painted-toenails—
Tsunami-mommy.

They'll giggle and scream
more than
they ever would
anywhere else.

Someone'll drop a popsicle
to the bottom.

Boxed time.

Two backyard fires:
      1. under tent
      above deck
      between beer bottles
      warmed in glow
      of circle flame;

      2. in our yard
      amid aged stone
      dated summers ago
      charred graham cracker brick
      sticky marshmallow spackle
      chocolate mouth corner—
      fingers licked clean,
      interlocked laughing;
            1. rainy nights
            blanket-hearth-home;

            2. starry metamorphosis
            peeper-summer-slumber-soundtrack;
Open-window-sleep
deeply;
cheap Moscato
lingers behind the toothpaste:
                We will die in this backyard—
                    hands open, eyes open—
                        starlight resting
                        cloudy vision—
                    still making s'mores
above ghosted body.

The Rain Has Taught Me How

        in sorrow
        beauty grows.

        Sadness
        ripens the roots
        with full bellies
        enlivening branches
        a deep sensual green.

As   the gutters drip
        the clouds puddle
        the sun washes its face of a blue sky,
        and *becomes* becoming of itself.

The earth = *richer.*
The air = *thicker.*
A smile = *strawberry-swollen-eyes.*

The rain has taught me how

trial is a shower
running through
mud-puddle crow's feet-footpaths,
dry cloth
wipes away underbrush—
thrusting roots deepening—
strengthen the hold
between rock, bone,
living once lived
down here.

The wisest teacher= *living itself.*

Through all things,
my roots are strong
flowers bloom,
but only with a *good* seasoning.

Kyle Potvin

Shun

[shoon] The Japanese tradition that food should be eaten only in its proper season, at peak flavor.

Tongue-tied blush
berry, rush
of ready
Nose of now
Slice crimson
Spoon cream
Tongue on June
Juice chin-loose
Sugar-tipped lip
Shun

Previously published in *Loosen*, Hobblebush Books, 2019

The Red Mooring Ball

The lake doesn't care that I stand on shore. It is busy
changing from gin to pelted to shimmer.

But the red mooring ball sees me. It waves and waves,
anchored until the water is drawn down for winter.

It floats out farther than where I can reach,
tendrils of plant life below teeming with August.

I could use the lush breaststroke of my youth. Chin in,
mouth closed, arms still strong.

Or turn on my back, body slicing straight through the crisp
water, trusting I know where to go.

Paula Puchala Timpson

See the Sea

I read about children
enjoying oranges for the first time
in a remote part of Alaska,
and how their joy was complete
within the simple scent of oranges
bright as life.
Imagine
children who
see the sea for the
first time,
hearts rushing open
to breathe in salty air and
taste all the love
blooming inside their hearts.
Gift given
received,
see the sea for the
first time and rejoice in
colors of heaven
creating
grace

Anna Schostak

Taboo

The classic story of a pair of friends
who fell in love without knowing them-
selves, or maybe, they wanted to pretend
a courtship wasn't blooming, just the stem.

In early summer, too much time spent to-
gether was taboo, as he was nine and
a half years her senior. Still they pursue
without support. It was hard to pretend

that their mutual trust and affection was not
obvious as they spent their walks at sun-
set sharing secrets. They both had the thought
that being together had just begun.

And then, they were standing under the moon
Kissing to the last sound of summer's tune.

Leslie Schultz

Rain Clouds to the East

The dawning light bounces, rosy and buoyant,
to the center of the sky, while off to the east
grey reigns, dragging its iron scepter—
ragged clouds, low and scudding—
over the auroran edge of the world.

Nearer, trees rise up like lollipops—
lime, white, pink, and red—buds tight
and dense as raindrops. At the street corner,
a stop sign stands like a cartoon tulip:
a sentry guarding the crossing
of one inscrutable season into another.

Meanwhile, as rain ticks against the windows,
lilacs distill their periwinkle, memorial fragrance.
Somewhere, cradled by twig, a blue-green egg waits.

Tiny Troubadour

This morning, mist hangs on the garden tree.
Our young wren, a bachelor, yearns near his house.
No lady has joined him, but he stays close,
guarding his nest, his round door with no key.

Each day, I watch him perched up on our fence,
near the wren house we hung from a newel post,
safe from stray cats. He sings and flits, looks lost
without a nesting mate. Yet, his competence

compels my human heart. Tiny stalwart,
his sentinel stance is so valiant and true.
He never abandons what he must pursue.
He continues to woo, though the warm months depart.

He continues to woo the late summer air,
over and over. No hint of despair.

Previously published in *Mezzo Cammin*

Silhouette: July Evening

At almost dusk, the garden fills
with small lights twinkling
among the flowering bee balm—
slick, lip-stick red—the popsicle-
bright orange of daylilies,
and ashy mauve, new-bloomed
hostas. Random and brief,
ignitions occur over impossibly
green lawns, seem caught
in low-hanging branches.

On the porch, in front of the dimming
white railing, quite near my chair,
I now see a flat, thin, dark body
floating. It's like a fragment of paper—
lofted char—perhaps a bit
of burnt manuscript,
still carrying a spark:
a flickering poem that insists,
intermittently
against the poet's will.

Pat Valdata

Shells

The soil here is full of shells,
whole neighborhoods built on calcium fill.

When we moved here, as I opened
each brown box, I found more: jars full,

from both coasts of Florida, all
the Jersey beaches of my childhood.

Who were these angelwings, cowries, cockles,
moon shells, oysters, whelks?

Common-as-dirt on my desk, a clamshell
holds paper clips in its purple bowl,

this skeleton shaped so differently from my own.

Previously published in *Glint*, Issue 10, Winter 2019

Aftermath

Beachcombing the shore where the Log Flume
used to be, who knows what we'll come upon?
Whelk shells, shark's teeth, shards of pottery
that once graced a dining table, photo frames
minus picture and glass. Waves still spume
toward the flattened dunes. What weather lottery
dropped this jetsam here? The boardwalk is gone.
No rides, no fries, no prizes. Who's to blame?

No matter how many sea walls they rebuild,
storms still flood mansion and bungalow;
no sand, no wind, no water can be willed
to stop a summer's littoral ebb and flow.
Shifting as designed, the barrier island
stays true to form. Nature isn't a villain.

Ocean City

A chocolate lab dashes
into and out of the waves, rubs
her belly and back along the wet
sand. I'd love to hug every

soggy inch of her. I remember
my first ocean: feet swept
by advancing foam, icy
swirl of salt under my heels,

surf booming in, hissing out,
the squeal of boardwalk rides,
lunch a cone of frozen custard
melting all over my hand.

We rode home with a towel
between the vinyl car seat
and our wet bathing suits,
sunburn flaming our arms.

Ryan Wasser

The Summer Hill

A thought for tonight—
just the *one*
among many.
Its worth far exceeds any number of pennies:
in front of me lies the hill of my youth,
not barren or dead;
it's a memory of summer, fresh honeysuckle
covered in dew while a sugar-sweet wind
blows and soothes
the fiercest burning in the depths
of my soul.
Like a film of my life, I watch from the Point:
all the good; all the bad;
my first kiss; my first fight,
and playing ball with the boys.
It's all gone today, and I can never go home
but the hill in my thoughts
will never grow old.

Previously published in *Reflections and Ruminations*, Raburn, 2014

Joyce Wilson

The Brook

I asked the brook to show
its knowledge of the world;
it raised the image of my face
but never said a word.

The shining surface trembled:
gnats rose up in swarms
like knotted iridescent strings
in effervescent storms.

My heart took flight and followed
into an open field
where amaranth and barley grew
and kestrels turned and wheeled.

And then I lost my way
upon a hard terrain
until I saw the brook emerge
and lead me on again.

Previously published in *Mezzo Cammin*

The Chickens

As morning breaks, they burst through open doors
like seltzer from a canister exploding.
They languish in the sandy dirt at noon.

An egg arrives, complete, and speckled brown.
One gray hen jumps and cackles for her egg;
another chatters out of sympathy.

Two reds extend a leg and then a wing
like prima ballerinas at the bar.
They stop formation to pursue a bug.

All tremble at a crossing thunderhead
as though their minds were fastened underground.
One jumps and flies against the flimsy fence.

They call softly to each other at dusk
and walk into their house in single file.
As roofs dissolve and blend into the night,

I wonder if their dreams are like their days,
a sisterhood of scratching in the sand;
then comes an egg, and then a falling sky.

Spittlebug
Cercopidae

While clinging to a reed beside the path,
it takes a morning glory bubble bath

and finds itself perfectible at home
spontaneously salivating foam.

And washing off unwanted dust and dirt
in a position seemingly inert,

creating bubbles in the summer air,
it gains renewal, simply sudsy there.

Previously published in *Ibbetson Street Magazine*

On the Beach

My solitude shimmers like a pearl,
opalescent in the winter sky.

Below, stones that have been thrown together,
as if against their will, heave suddenly;

their shadows reach beyond their huddled shapes,
their stubborn selves, exaggerating them.

In changing surfaces of softened ground,
I seek treasures, origins, what I first

thought, or what I thought I might have meant.
One glimmers like a mollusk in the tides.

How close the words: treasure and erasure.
A wave across the sand removes debris,

the signs made by the patterns of my feet.
Then a million bubbles fill and gasp.

SUMMERTIME STORIES

John Abernethy

Helter-Skelter

Helterskelterinasummerswelter . . . the words on the page melt together like gooey fudge in the Fourth of July sun. "Dude, you read way too much for what's good for you," Quentin comments. I'm lying face-down on my seriously-frayed Spiderman beach towel that I'd probably had since fifth grade.

Cold waves collapse onto the white-hot beach at Asbury Park, dissolving castles and child-dug moats, before retreating with a sigh of resignation. The sand is everywhere, especially in my butt crack. I really hate sand. I look up from my book and over my shades at my friend Quentin. His face and chest are pockmarked with bright red splotches of acne and sunburn. Later tonight, I think, he's going to be one sore dude. "What's up, Q.T.?"

Quentin looks away. I follow his eyes which are tracking two girls about our age walking along the smooth, wet sand at the shore line. Tan and lithe, they glide indifferently between raucous scrums of younger kids skittering across the water on their boogie boards. It's impossible to look away. "Let's get in the water," Quentin says without looking at me. "I'm frying out here."

I shut my book and stand up, brushing the sand off my board shorts and arms. Kicking my wallet further underneath my beach towel, I toss my t-shirt over my new Vans. They were too expensive to have some Pez head boost them while we're in the water. "OK, I'm ready when you are."

As the girls retreat down the beach, Quentin's eyes are locked onto them like a pair of heat-seeking missiles. I know he hasn't heard a word I've said. "Q.T.!" I say, poking a toe into his outstretched foot. "Q! Let's go. Water. Cool off. Remember?"

Quentin jumps up and begins a slow jog across the beach in a diagonal line toward the girls and the water. I start after him, hopping every few steps to avoid the white-hot sand. We head on a course to cross in front of the girls and I reflexively suck in my stomach. As we lope past, I can hear them laughing. The sound makes me happy.

Quentin and I splash into the water and dive under a fat, breaking wave. The water is biting cold and salty. As we break the surface, I shake the water and sand out of my hair and notice the seawater glide off my skin, reminding me of a porpoise. We swim out just over our heads, beyond the breaking waves and most of the crowd, treading water with the rise and fall of the rolling surface. "This is awesome," I say to Quentin. We've been coming to the beach together for a week every July 4th since we were eight. Quentin's parents have a beach house.

"Yeah, it's pretty cool," he replies with a wry grin. Laughing, he palms a handful of water into my face. Sputtering, I retaliate by jumping on his shoulders, pushing him under the water. When he breaks the surface, we start a frenzied fight of splashing each other until we are both out of breath. Quentin hoots and slaps both hands into the water sending up sprays of sparkling water like an exploding seltzer bottle. I lay back in the water and float, looking up into a cloudless blue sky. With my ears under water, there's a deep silence. I listen to my own breathing and the liquidly sound of Quentin paddling nearby.

I have a vague memory of being on the beach when I am much younger. My dad stands next to me. On the sand, a lifeguard in red trunks breathes air into the mouth of a kid. Each time he stops to press rhythmically on his chest with crossed palms, I notice the kid's blue lips. I can't look away. The lifeguard's offering encouragement to the kid, or maybe himself. "Com'on, you can do it! You can do it!"

Gabriel

Sitting far back under the boardwalk, Gabriel leans back against a makeshift recliner of black trash bags stuffed with his clothes. Sighing with contentment, the whisper of the sea in the distance and the cool sand beneath him, he reaches into the box of books at his side. He hears the steady tread of footfalls of families strolling on the boardwalk above him and chooses a well-worn copy of Camus' *L'Etranger*. His lips move as he quietly begins to read, feeling a gourmand's pleasure as the melodic words gambol over his tongue like french wine and escargot.

Aujourd'hui, maman est morte. Ou peut-être hier, je ne sais pas. J'ai reçu un télégramme de l'asile : « Mère décédée. Enterrement de- main. Sentiments distingués. » Cela ne veut rien dire. C'était peut- être hier. Despite the delicious quiet and solitude of the space, he knows he'll need to find another place to wait out the fireworks which will ravage the night air later that night. Even as a child, he hated fireworks, the helter-skelter smash of garish colors and the searing detonation of acrid gunpowder. It confounds him like a strobe light abuses an epileptic; he can't sleep or think clearly for days afterward, his mind distorted like a Kandinsky painting.

Exhaling sadly, he closes his book and drops it back into his ersatz library. He stands up, careful to avoid bumping his head, and, stooping, begins to scuttle across the sand towards the edge of the boardwalk. Wary of being seen, he keeps a watchful eye for anyone on the beach who might be looking back. Emerging into the harsh sunlight, he turns immediately to his right and follows the edge of the boardwalk towards a flight of stairs. As he begins the slow upward climb, he's startled by two boys bounding past him.

"D'yah check out that perv we just passed?" Quentin asks in a low whisper, leaning across as we walk quickly down the boardwalk. "Creepy."

"Yeah, somethin' must be wrong with him," I answer warily. I sneak a look back at the old man wearing a bright-blue baseball cap and a grunt-load of clothes, way too much for a hot day in July.

———————————

Stepping out of the shower at Quentin's house, I grab a towel and start to dry off. The shower's brought out the sunburn, and my skin is becoming sore. Wiping the steam off the mirror over the sink, I'm startled by two white circles circling my eyes where my sunglasses have been. "Great, I look like a fuckin' raccoon."

Moaning, I walk back into the bedroom. Quentin's propped up on one of the beds, eyes closed, mouthing words to music I can't hear. I lift an ear of his headphones to listen.

"Rap crap," I critique, letting the earpiece snap back into place. Quentin looks up and frowns. Actually, I like most rap music but pretend not to. We both enjoy giving each other a hard time; it's part of our bromance. He disses me about my big nose and funny walk. I pretended I don't think his mom is hot.

The Boardwalk

Gabriel trembles violently in the darkness, his back pressed up against a side wall of the Palace Arcade. He's hidden from view behind a dented trash can shaped like a lurid circus clown. Earlier that evening, while searching out a quiet place in the alley to wait out the fireworks, someone shoved him against a metal dumpster. "Gimme your wallet, freak!" the dark figure screamed, splattering his face with spit. Grabbing it, he laughed as he smashed Gabriel's face against the metal container, igniting stabbing hot shards of light in his brain.

After dinner with Quentin's parents and younger sister, we head out for a night of teenage debauchery. The night air and ocean breeze blow away the summer heat, raising goosebumps on my exposed arms. The boardwalk vibrates with the stripping sounds and shuffling of a thousand feet. Shrieks from amusement park rides and pulsing carnival light strobes propel the crowd along. Quentin and I trail a pair of girls walking arm in arm just ahead of us, their heads popping up and down, their jean bottoms just covering their butts.

"I think it's them," Quentin shouts at me over the din of the crowd, "the girls from the beach today!" It's like we already know them. "What are we going to say?" I ask nervously. Quentin shakes his head, grinning wildly.

"I gotta get rid of my trash first," I shout. I was carrying a pretzel wrapper and the bottom tip of an ice cream cone. I pointed over to a trash can by the arcade wall. Quentin nods his head but doesn't look at me. "Hurry up; I'll keep them in sight."

Slipping through the crowd, I reach the trash can and shove my junk into its clown-faced mouth, wiping my sticky palms down my shorts. Beside the can, I see the crumpled figure of the creepy guy from the beach, a bleeding slash of flesh across his cheek. He reaches out a shaking hand towards me as I recoil. "Shit!" I cry out, freaked by his wild hair and empty expression. He looks like Charles Manson.

Suddenly, I feel panicked and untethered, disoriented by the flashing lights, and weirdly disembodied. I lurch recklessly back through the pulsing crowd, trying to catch a reassuring glimpse of Quentin somewhere ahead of me. I feel the chill of the deep ocean pulling at me, my toes struggling to find the sand below the water. I can't seem to catch my breath. I'm going to pass out.

Louis Daily

Our Last Summer

(Based on an actual dream)

I remember it rained a lot that summer. Especially the day I met you.

I stood outside with my hands in my pockets and my hair plastered sheepishly to my forehead, staring up at the sign hanging down from the awning. Bella's Corner.

A couple walked by me, cowering together beneath an umbrella. Both of them looked me up and down judgmentally as even they passed under the broad awning. I blinked away the rain, wanting to call after them, 'it's just a little water' or something. But I withheld, basking in the fact that this was in fact probably helping me deal with the humidity, so the joke was on them.

I entered the café.

Inside, there were a lot of green plants, a good number of which were lined up along the right-hand windowsill, exotically blocking out most of a quaint street-view. There were a handful of tables beside this; one was occupied by two men in their late thirties/early forties who looked like they would belong at a truck-stop bar. The one facing me gave me a wave.

Otherwise, it was your typical small and cluttered, low-lit hipster dive. Not loud, although something familiar was quietly playing on the radio:

See that girl, watch that scene. Diggin' the Dancing Queen

No one was behind the counter, so I took a moment to examine my drink choices on the chalkboard hanging on the wall:

Sad Zebra Frappuccino – A fresh blend of iced mocha with stripes of vanilla and chocolate syrup.

Cool Cat Frap. – Same thing, but with caramel. Meow.

Bella's Secret Brew - ???

Dumbfounded, I simply could not make up my mind. I knew I needed caffeine, though, or else I would likely collapse on the floor right then and there.

That was when you came out from the back. You looked so familiar. Your dimpled smile was quite wry, almost a grimace. Your hair was cropped short and tousled-looking, and you had a nose ring. You were wearing a checkered apron with a green shirt underneath with words that were too covered-up to read. I might have been able to catch on to what it said, but I didn't want you to think my gaze was lingering . . . well . . . too low beneath your face, so instead I found myself in an impromptu staring-contest with your gray eyes. You won.

I didn't know what to say, so I said,

"Are you…Bella?"

You narrowed your eyes at me and pointed to your name tag, which I would have seen if I wasn't such an idiot.

"Oh, I guess not…" I said. "Do you know what's in Bella's Secret?"

You bit your lip. "What do you think?"

She works here, you dumbass, I thought to myself.

"Okay, I'll try that," I decided.

"Coming right up." And then you turned to blend my drink. Whatever it was.

I went to take a seat, trying not to get too close to the "truckers." I could have sworn they were watching and laughing at me. But then again, they might have just been dancing in their seats to the disco music that was still playing. I sat facing away from them and twiddled my thumbs, anxiously waiting for my drink.

"Personally, I think 'Our Last Summer' is their best song," I overheard one of the truckers say. And then he started humming a tune, quite well, I might add. It was a romantic melody, fitting for the season, I thought, as well as for a cup of coffee. I decided these guys were probably alright.

Just as the man started singing—something like, "walks alone insane" (which I would later learn was walks along the Seine, as in the river in France), you appeared before me with my drink.

"One Bella's Secret," you said, placing on the table before me.

"Thanks," I said, scrutinizing the dark contents of my cup.

I could sense you were looking down at me. I slowly lifted my face to look, nervous at what your expression might have been. But to my surprise, you were looking past the edge of the table at my feet.

"Nice boots," you said.

"Oh . . . thanks," I said, feeling my cheeks start burning, and not just from the coffee.

I could sense the truckers behind me turning to admire my boots as well.

Your demeanor was suddenly a lot more cheerful, I thought. "Are they new?"

"Yeah, I literally just bought them."

"Nice."

You cocked your head thoughtfully and turned to go. Now I was the one grimacing as I sat there sipping some sort of motor fuel, watching your back, wishing you would turn around again.

Which you did, just as the radio went quiet and you had fixed yourself a cold beverage.

"You know, today would be a good day to break those suckers in."

"Huh?"

Then you finally asked me for my name.

We talked some more, and I gathered that you really liked hiking. It was like you were itching to get outside even though it was raining. I realized I felt the same way. I'd been cooped up at home for so long, after all. A hike in the rain might be nice.

I went for it.

"Alright then. How 'bout we go for a walk?"

You searched my face quizzically as you fiddled with your empty mug. "A walk, huh?"

"Sure."

You checked your watch. "Morning shift's almost over. I get off in like twenty minutes. Think you can wait up?"

"Definitely."

"Cool beans."

I unlocked the car. We both got in and were silent for a moment. I could feel your eyes on mine as I stared out through the windshield.

I switched on the engine. I noticed I was low on fuel.

"I have to stop for gas first," I told you.

You shrugged. "No prob. There's something I wanna pick up at the gas station anyway."

"Like what?"

"You'll see."

"Okay."

I followed you into the minimart. You got straight in line for the cashier—which meant you went straight to the cashier because there was no line.

You spoke to the cashier from behind the plexiglass:

"Two Powerball tickets."

He went to take them down from the wall.

"Lottery tickets?" I questioned. "That's what you wanted to get?"

You shrugged. "Well yeah. You said you lost your job, right?"

"Well . . . yeah . . ."

"And I, like, need something to look forward to for a change. I dunno. My treat."

"Oh . . . okay. Thanks."

The man came back and slid our tickets under the small hole beneath the plexiglass. You paid and handed me my ticket. As we stepped away from the counter, though, you stopped me before I could begin to even scratch off one number.

"Not yet," you told me. "Let's just wait. Until tonight. That way we'll be able to have hope all day."

I thought to myself, you must be really patient. Which, judging by everything else about you came as a surprise.

"Oh, okay. But aren't you curious if I win? Or don't you think I'd be curious if you did?"

"What's your point?"

"I mean . . . will we even be together at the end of the day?"

You cocked your head. "Maybe it's best we don't find out what each other got," you decided.

I was kind of hoping your response would be, 'Of course we will.'

I shook my head and smiled. "Whatever. You do know what the chances are of winning these things anyway, right?"

"Never tell me the odds!" you said, channeling Han Solo.

I parked somewhere along the creek. Our feet crunched along the gravel.

We crested a hill where the trees on the left thinned into a clearing. Vertical clouds streamed the sky to the horizon. As gray as the sky was, there was an undercurrent of bright colors that cast us in a hazy spotlight. I looked over at you and saw that your face was lit in a warm glow as you squinted upward. For the first time, I looked at your feet to examine what you yourself were wearing: beat-up old chucks with high socks.

We continued along the path, the open green expanse always at our side. The music of the cicadas kept us company; at times, you hummed your own little tune. I couldn't tell what it was, and I didn't ask.

We came across a bench to the right, amidst a line of trees. Without question, you sat down. I settled onto the bench a few feet next to you. You leaned against the back with your arms crossed, I sat forward with my hands folded, and there we were, staring out at a field of tall grass under a sky like murky waters.

"Have you ever walked this far?" you finally asked.

I shrugged. "Probably. I come to this trail a lot. It's been a while, though."

We listened to the crescendo of the cicadas once again.

"Thank you," you said. "I've been waiting so long for . . . something like this."

I noticed you were smiling sadly now.

"Of course." I thought of what to say next. "How long have you worked at Bella's?"

You shrugged. "I don't even know anymore. But I do like it there."

"That's good."

You bit your lip. "It's all I do anymore, though."

"Oh . . . sorry."

"It's cool."

To my surprise, you slid over and rested your head on my shoulder. I stiffened. You noticed and looked up at me.

"Sorry."

I shook my head. "No big deal."

"I was just a little tired."

"Oh, okay." I smiled.

You laid your head back down and closed your eyes.

You started humming again, and it reminded me of that ABBA song the guy back at the café had been singing. It made me feel sad, yet present, and maybe even lucky, for the first time in recent memory.

Ian Kertis

The Quique Gang

"Delaware with Dad" was not necessarily summer in Spain. Nonetheless, Xander awaited his father, scanning the distance like a bird on a telephone wire to catch the wavy, dark green Impreza, its outline gliding out of the horizon, floating up the hilly cul-de-sac, and at last, bending itself into the driveway. On the threshold, Dad—the swarthy, smiling, almond-eyed man known to his friends as "Quique"—would greet Xander with a powerful hug and Xander's mother with a warm but old smile. A couple minutes' airy chat. This year, Quique lingered longer than usual in conversation. His eyes had a soft, slightly cloudy glint.

"Remember Mr. Frothy?" he offered apropos of nothing. Xander did, and so did his mother, judging by the surprised chuckle and knowing grin she quickly stifled. Mr. Frothy was a purple, orange-spotted Tyrannosaurus rex. His claws were conspicuously turquoise, yellow, and lilac. Xander hadn't seen these claws in years, but he had a flickering, soft-focus memory of prodding and purring at his mother until she colored them with her fingernail varnish.

"I thought we lost him ages ago," said his mother in her characteristic flat murmur. Quique shook his head and twitched his black eyebrows conspiratorially.

"I found him in the garage when I was packing beach stuff."

"I'll bet he's ready for a fresh manicure," she replied. Xander couldn't help looking down at the driveway, hoping his cheeks weren't burning too brightly at the reminder of his childhood fancy. Quique seemed to recognize the signs of budding teenage embarrassment and gave him a quick, soft hand on the shoulder, an effort to lightly reassure Xander of the cocoon of fatherly pride and affection that Mr. Frothy was in no danger whatsoever of puncturing.

"Do you want to see him—he's in the trunk?"

"No, thanks." Xander's mother cast a quick, sensitive glance his direction. "I won't keep you from your travels." And with that, the exchange was largely at an end and the journey set to begin.

Xander always experienced the long highway drive to Rehoboth Beach in an altered state of consciousness: a shivery, green-tinged panorama dipping him in and out of queasy sleep to a soundtrack of hissing air-conditioner and "Dear Mr. Fantasy." The leaking sole of Dave Mason's shoe seemed to be the surface of Xander's brain. But at journey's end there was the turquoise ocean air and grey seagulls with their yellow trumpeting beaks at full volume across the sky, consuming whatever they pleased to assuage their hunger. There were hot sand and red-cold cherry water ice that stained Xander's lips and tongue.

There were Paul and Jamie, of course, and this year they had bought a big new umbrella. They planted it firmly in the sand. Its Roy G. Biv vertical stripes arched from their center point toward the glistening, rolling shore. A fringe of little white frills danced in the breeze.

While Xander sat on the yellow-and-scarlet blanket in the shade of the umbrella, he watched the sky through the bars of color encircling him. Puffing wind, jumping waves, and soaking sun were at play. He could hear their three-way and looked out across the uneven turrets of sand, the rows of iceboxes, canvas chairs, and parasols, to the water welding particles of earth and stretching out to the invisible, yearning, and vivid distance.

As he lay there, Xander's mind inevitably fluttered back to his first Rehoboth summer with the Quique Gang. He must have been six or eight then—soft-serve ice cream and the big, Christmas tree-colored Ferris wheel the pinnacle of ecstasy. He retained as well a vision of Jamie experimenting with a pair of psychedelic fairy wings, a novelty someone had managed to locate at a boardwalk shop while Xander was trying for new swimming trunks. Xander had settled on purple, a dark juicy shade that illuminated his pale legs in what he would later learn was an excellent instance of simultaneous contrast—his body a moving canvas on which to splash color and play at chiaroscuro. At the time, he'd viewed himself in the long mirror with a confusing ambivalence, feeling like a wooden chair someone had forgotten (or decided not) to give a final coat of varnish.

Jamie was a big sort of man, all black hair and muscle. With his beach tan in place, his arms looked a lot like two well-baked loaves of homemade bread. Wearing his cinnamon-red trunks, he had strapped the translucent wings over his shiny wet shoulders— parading along the beach, stopping to socialize with various other shiny bread-loaf men. Standing on the water's edge, Jamie would point at his wings and laugh uproariously. The man he was laughing with whacked his ass lightly with a dark blue boogie board, and Jamie laughed some more and strode on to engage a nearby glistening lifeguard with his toothy grin.

Xander felt a little more at home with Paul, a comparatively slight man who shared some of Xander's unvarnished chair look. Each summer, Paul sprayed sunblock on Xander's belly and back. The spray was cool and made him want to laugh. Paul always smiled, catching Xander's response from the corner of his eye, and then handed him a bottle of cream so he could rub some on his nose and cheeks. Paul, who preferred not to be whacked on the ass with any wet, sandy accessories, handled sunscreen and other frilly details. Jamie, who could sunbathe in almost any weather and worked nights at one of the restaurants not far off the boardwalk (Xander had never eaten there), rented the house. Xander's dad was something of a ringmaster: corralling divergent factions, reeling in Jamie's spicy acrobatics, drawing Paul out of his quiet fussiness, and steering Xander down the middle while attending (Xander would later realize) to the various, evolving needs and amusements of an evolving, variant boy.

That first summer, though, had been the Year of the Fruit Hat: a spectacular, hilariously too-large sunhat Xander's father had dropped over his head. Floppy and wide, the hat was so decorated with patterns of fruit (watermelon, banana, berry bursting out of a magenta fabric) that even when Xander was six, it reminded him of Carmen Miranda movies his grandparents had shown him.

"Where'd you get that?" Paul asked

"Colorful, Caribbean-themed place down the boardwalk." Xander's father sat on a low canvas chair beside Paul, stretched his legs out, and leaned in close. Xander pulled the wide brim of his hat down and lay back on the blanket.

"Hey!" Jamie's voice billowed up, waking Xander. He stretched in the heat, lifted his hat, and sat up. "Are you guys ever comin' in!?! The water's great waves are really movin'!" A flipbook, a sequence of stop motion shots: Jamie rushing back down to the water's edge, his fairy wings flapping, glittering, and dripping with water. Quique rising with a smile and taking Paul by the arm. Paul turning over his shoulder and beckoning to Xander with his wide, pale palm.

Then they were up to their ankles. Cold water spitting on the sand. The ground parting under their feet into islands: Jamie flying far away, his arms outstretched to the sun, fairy wings standing erect on his shoulders; Paul and Quique sharing a patch of sand, balancing on each other. Fairy wings off somewhere, floating on the blue distance.

Xander's hair in his eyes, battered by the wind. A wall of water erupting in front of him, pushing and spinning, surrounding him. Paul staggering; Paul's arm; Xander losing the arm as they both lost their legs. Sound died as he lay flat on the sand.

A vision of himself: half conscious—sleep paralysis—skin empty—motionless below the sea. The wall of water filling his eyes.

A violent silver blur. His body flying up into the sun. Olive arms holding him still, hoisting him to shore and trying to stand him up as his legs shook giddily. By the time he regained awareness, the wave had vanished.

Even now, seven years later and at the age of twelve and two months, when he lay on the same shore and closed his eyes, Xander inevitably met the massive wave crashing down over him. He tried instead to imagine the swinging ocean as a huge, soft lap he fell into while the arms of the wind caressed him, but as the waves tossed him, it was difficult to tell where water ended and sky began, so he was lost again, tumbling through a seamless horizon of blue. The blue arched, sending him down-down-down until he landed once more on warm sand. To one side, the ocean was just near enough for trails of saltwater to inch their way between his toes and tickle him intermittently. On the other, scattered stones on the shore stretched to the feet of grey, jagged mountains. He felt the cliffs' shadows protecting him, and above this, a sky of many colors, its thin, streaky clouds taking on the hues of the striped umbrella and dancing before his eyes like the Aurora Borealis magnified into a circus tent.

Feeling something poking out of the sand under his ears, Xander reached back and pulled out a small, shiny plastic body. He recognized its texture in his hands and, from the corner of his eye, bright-tinted chips of nail varnish it shed onto the beach. Xander turned his head, resting one cheek against the sand to gaze at his buried treasure. There, at last unimpeded, his claws glistening and his arms outstretched in a great embrace, Mr. Frothy reached up to Xander.

Dan Lonsdale

The Tooth

You sit and stare out at the ocean from your beach towel, your hand mindlessly running through the warm sand. Your gaze locks with the horizon, the point where the sea seeks to challenge the sky for supremacy. You feel the fear simmer in your stomach but are unable to look away.

Your parents don't understand this fear. They wonder how a young boy could go from gleefully riding waves on his boogie board one day to avoiding the water completely the next. How could their son look out at all of the other kids splashing and playing in the surf and not want to join in?

What they don't understand is that you didn't have all the information. You weren't as wise as you are now. Once you know about all that's out there, how could you even consider putting another toe into that kind of danger?

It all started with that stupid necklace your grandmother bought you from the gift shop the day before. Dozens of them sat at the checkout counter, teasing every customer to make another impulse buy before the end of the season. It certainly caught your eye. Smooth, white, and sharp enough to cut your finger if you pressed down firmly.

"Great choice there, little man," exclaimed the cashier, "Ladies will love the way that thing looks and it's on sale for only ten dollars."

Your grandmother glanced over, immediately seeing your fixation with it. She smiled and remarked, "When I was a little girl, my brother and I would comb the beaches looking for teeth just like these. We searched for hours until we found a few big enough to sell to the boardwalk shops. Then, they would turn them into these."

She pulled one down from the rack, "This is a big one, maybe from a tiger shark." You looked over at her, puzzled. "There are different kinds of sharks?"

"Oh yes, many different ones," she answered, "Tiger sharks, bull sharks, hammerhead sharks, and of course Great Whites. You know, like the one from Jaws."

Although you had never seen the movie, you nodded back at her, eyes filled with wonder. Sensing your peaked interest, she turned toward the cashier and pulled her wallet out of her purse. Moments later, the two of you walked out of the store, the shark tooth resting comfortably below your throat.

Later that evening, you jumped on your iPad and began searching for everything you could find about the original owner of your newest prized possession. You started by comparing the tooth around your neck to different charts, trying to find an exact match. Before you knew it, you had gone down the rabbit hole. You found information about all of the different types your grandmother had mentioned earlier. You read page after page on Wikipedia as your mind begins to fill with information on different lengths, weights, and prey. You went deeper, watching YouTube clips and old National Geographic videos that show sharks breaching high above the sea, snatching seals with their giant, toothy mouths. This was when the first flames of fear began to ignite in your gut. Words seem to hide the violence of nature in a way that video never can.

Still, you kept searching, way too far down into the hole to stop. Then, you found it. The page that turned your fear from a match into a bonfire. You had been coming down to the Jersey shore your entire life and you had never once heard about it. The Shark Attacks of 1916.

The first attack happened to a man who was 23 years old. He was playing with his dog in the ocean, just like you had seen so many others do. The shark bit his leg, right on the thigh. At first, other people on the beach thought he was just calling for the dog to join him in the water. By the time they realized he was injured, it was too late. He bled to death in a nearby hotel.

Five days later, another attack. Another man in his twenties. The shark severed his legs from his body. He died as lifeguards tried to bring him ashore. You absorbed this information in a state of shock, but you could not bring yourself to stop reading on.

The third attack is the one that brought you to your breaking point. This time it was a boy. He was 11, just a year younger than you. He wasn't even in the ocean but in a nearby creek, playing with his friends. They saw the dorsal fin coming towards them in the water. They scattered, trying to get away. The shark grabbed the unlucky boy and dragged him below. They found his body two days later downstream.

The iPad tumbled from your hands to the floor, your entire body trembling. To some, it might have seemed like ancient history. But when you can hear that same ocean from your bedroom, when you spent the day in that same water where those people died, history has a way of quickly coming back to life.

You wanted to take off the tooth, still hung on the cheap string around your neck. You wanted to rip it off and throw it back into the ocean where it belongs. Instead, you stared up at the ceiling of your dark bedroom, unable to sleep. Your fingers still tracing the sharp edges, imagining the hundreds of other teeth in the mouth of the great, monstrous beast.

The next day you return to the beach, but not to the ocean. You sit and stare out at the ocean from your beach towel, your hand mindlessly running through the warm sand. The fear still runs cold throughout every inch of your body. You continue to stare out at the dark water as if you expect them to appear at any minute. To show themselves, to mark their territory, to let everyone else know the same terror you feel in your gut.

Yet, everyone else acts as nothing could be better. The warm sunshine and cool breeze from the sea bring a wonderful comfort to all of the beachgoers around you. You see a few boys about your age that are throwing a football around and making diving catches into the surf. A few boogie boarders desperately trying to catch every strong wave that comes their way. Despite how fun everything looks, you can't bring yourself to rise from your beach towel.

Then it happens. You hear the scream—a muffled cry for help. You see everyone's heads snap towards the ocean. You look for the dorsal fin, the dark shadow below the water, the bright red cloud of blood staining the sea. Instead, you see something else.

You see a woman is standing at the shoreline screaming and pointing out towards the ocean. She isn't pointing at a monster but a boy. He's younger than you, maybe seven or eight. You see his head bobbing up and down. His arms flailing up towards the sky.

From where you are sitting, it looks like he is being sucked into the middle of the ocean like the sea is claiming him for its own. He drifts further and further away until his head slips below the surface—the boy's mother shrieks.

You rise from your beach towel to take in this new horror. This new fear that water has in store for you. An endless power that runs as deep as the ocean floor. Despite the horror that grips you now, you cannot look away. You can never look away.

A flash of red flies across your field of vision. It's a young woman sprinting, as fast as her feet can carry her, past the crying mother and into the surf. She dives, headfirst into an oncoming wave, paddling and kicking against the strength of the sea. At the point where the boy disappeared, she goes under. Gone.

Your eyes are locked, unblinking, on the spot she went under. Each second that goes by feels like a year. Suddenly, she rises out of the wave, breaching the surface just like the Great Whites off the shore of Seal Island, the boy clutched between her arms. She takes him and paddles sideways, down the shoreline until finally turning towards the safety of the beach. The boy is crying, gasping for air, but very much alive.

The boy's mother is there next. She is still crying as she squeezes her son. The woman in the red bathing suit stays with them. The mother thanks her over and over again, struggling to say much of anything else. The young woman simply nods and smiles before crouching back to talk to the boy. She gestures towards the water and then shoreline, explaining something, unraveling a secret of the water. The boy nods his head, listening as best as one can after such an experience. Then, the young woman in red turns and heads back toward her giant white throne.

You gaze at her for a while as she takes her seat and begins to twirls a whistle between her fingers. She stares back out at the water. Then, you do the same. You take a step from your beach towel. Then, another. You stop at the edge of the water. Your toes feeling the cool, foamy ripples of the sea.

Julia Otto

Average

Middle-class salary measured by % of those attaining it or the wish of financial and familial security or maybe a successful career or a place to live alone or a new story to tell or it's just getting the opportunity to wish on a weed like trying to wear too-high-shoes and buying them anyways because you look *damn good* and knowing that one day you may never wear them but that's okay because it'll always be tucked under the bed like an old stuffed toy that you used to play in fake houseplants with and read the bible to like a shopping list while church rung around you grew up into where you are you silly thing but that's okay because it's attainable sometimes you have to try to fail to get anywhere and even when you're there it's not *quite* looking like the topside of a new penny but like a sun-bleached plastic horse stuck in the earth from a childhood left behind you remember this when the rain washes the grass to mud and you pull it up with old scissors that you used to cut the grass when Mom was mowing you kept yourself busy and didn't realize all you had and all you didn't, hell— you ate every day and had mac and cheese for breakfast sometimes and had a shirt with *best friends* on it and pictures of peanut-butter-jelly, you smiled a lot and cried alone and it was a domesticated cat of a childhood and that's all you can ask for is knowing that debt isn't a friend but a coworker you need to smile at and that it'll always be there even when you call out sick but it's okay to call out sick and go to the beach because it's how you'll keep lung in your airs you'd be a deflated birthday if you didn't do that every once in a-while and sometimes you kept little fish in a tank that were neon pink and orange they had hundreds of babies that one time, we caught them all but they all died from the *bubbling disease* you still don't know why but it was amazing to realize that sex was innate and that babies came from all places you didn't know that your cousins weren't your cousins until you left a Valentines party with sweets in your lap and your mom explained how you weren't related just *"close friends"* and you asked how many and she said three families and you went from thirteen cousins to two but still you're related *you know?* because you grew up together and threw blocks at each other in the basement, you all played the same games and hated and loved each other the same it's that tolerance you have when your parents are all friends, and you can sit at the lunch table and talk about nothing or just eat the vegetable spread you visit each other's grad parties even if you don't know who they are anymore you still bring a gift straight from work because your mom said to go it's like being sick on Christmas and going to the last Urgent Care and getting antibiotics because *where did this bronchitis come from* but it's okay because you can breathe by New Years and laugh a few days after before school starts you have new jeans to wear through the snow you feel well-dressed and awkward, and that's how you'll live until you can convince yourself to get a tattoo you study what your parents do in college even if you want to do something else because dreams are the backburners of reality and reality is how we all get fed.

ABOUT THE AUTHORS

John Abernethy has an M.A. in Creative Writing. He lives outside West Chester, PA, with his wife (whom he met in a tenth-grade biology lab) and dog(s). He was first bitten by a love of creative writing after winning a prestigious award with a brilliant story about robots in Mr. Pitt's sixth-grade class writing contest. He thinks his dog ate it afterward. John and his wife love to read, travel, and listen to music (although they disagree about the genre and volume). Sitting beside the ocean, eating, and wearing funny socks are also passions. John loves to drive unreliable British cars (his first was an MGB GT) and write amusing Christmas letters to entertain his friends.

Vincent Carcirieri is pursuing his master's degree in English literature at West Chester University. He has written for other publications, such as West Chester's own *Quad* and the Intercollegiate Studies Institute's *Intercollegiate Review*.

Terese Coe's poems and translations appear in *Agenda; Alaska Quarterly Review; Cincinnati Review; Crannog; Hopkins Review; Metamorphoses; The Moth; New American Writing; New Scotland Writing; Ploughshares; Poetry; Poetry Review; The Stinging Fly; The Threepenny Review,* and the *TLS*, among dozens of others. Her collection *Shot Silk* was short-listed for the 2017 Poets Prize, and her latest collection *Why You Can't Go Home Again*, was published by Kelsay Books in 2018. Her poem "More" was heli-dropped across London in the "Rain of Poems" for the 2012 Olympics. The poems in this text, "Courage of a Poet" and "As Wild as We," were first published in *Orchards* and *Miller's Pond Annual,* respectively.

Barbara Crooker is a poetry editor for *Italian-Americana,* and author of twelve chapbooks and nine full-length books of poetry. *Some Glad Morning,* Pitt Poetry Series, University of Pittsburgh Poetry Press, 2019, is the latest. Her awards include the WB Yeats Society of New York Award, the Thomas Merton Poetry of the Sacred Award, and three Pennsylvania Council on the Arts Creative Writing Fellowships. Her work appears in a variety of literary journals and anthologies, including *The Valparaiso Poetry Review, The Chariton Poetry Review, Green Mountains Review, Tar River Poetry Review, The Hollins Critic, The Denver Quarterly, Christianity and Literature, The American Poetry Journal, Passages North, Nimrod, Common Wealth: Contemporary Poets on Pennsylvania, The Bedford Introduction to Literature, Nasty Women: An Unapologetic Anthology of Subversive Verse,* and has been read on the ABC, the BBC, *The Writer's Almanac, The Slowdown,* and featured on Ted Kooser's *American Life in Poetry.*

Louis Daily is a two-time graduate of West Chester University with both Bachelor's and Master's degrees in English. He is a lifelong resident of the Philadelphia area, where he acts in and directs theatrical and musical productions. These days he can mostly be found working the cafe at Barnes & Noble, which he loves due to being surrounded by books. Louis is an aspiring fantasy novelist and hopes to have his urban fairy tales published one day. He is thrilled to share an excerpt from his short story *Our Last Summer* with you in this publication.

Charlotte Innes is the author of *Descanso Drive,* a book of poems (Kelsay Books) and two poetry chapbooks, *Licking the Serpent* and *Reading Ruskin in Los Angeles,* both published by Finishing Line Press. Her poems have appeared in many publications, including *The Hudson Review, The Sewanee Review, Tampa Review, Rattle, Valparaiso Poetry Review, The High Window* (U.K.), and a number of anthologies, including *Wide Awake: Poets of Los Angeles and Beyond (*Beyond Baroque Books, 2015) and *The Best American Spiritual Writing for 2006* (Houghton writer for many publications including *The Nation* and the *Los*

Angeles Times, she currently tutors students in English and creative writing. Originally from England, Charlotte Innes now lives in Los Angeles.

Karen Kelsay is the editor at Kelsay Books, a poetry publishing company based in Utah. Her poems have appeared in several hundred journals.

Ian Kertis is a West Chester University graduate student, Greater Philly Area native, and writer of fiction (and occasionally other strange and hopefully successful hybrid forms). With an accent on queer themes, Ian strives to create prose lyric imagery that tells stories he hopes will prove to be immersive for all readers (queer or otherwise). His wish is for readers to discover and experience more from his work than he alone can imagine.

Jean L. Kreiling is the author of two collections of poetry: *Arts & Letters & Love* (2018) and *The Truth in Dissonance* (2014). Her work has been honored with the *Able Muse Write* Prize, the Great Lakes Commonwealth of Letters Sonnet Prize, the Kelsay Books Metrical Poetry Prize, a Laureates' Prize in the Maria W. Faust Sonnet Contest, three New England Poetry Club prizes, the Plymouth Poetry Contest prize, and the *String Poet* Prize. Kreiling is Professor Emeritus of Music at Bridgewater State University; her articles on the intersections between music and literature have been published in several academic journals. Note: Childe Hassam's "Summer Evening" can be found at https://florencegriswoldmuseum.org/collections/online/foxchase/fo x-chase-childe-hassam/.

Jenna Le is the author of *Six Rivers* (NYQ Books, 2011) and *A History of the Cetacean American Diaspora* (Indolent Books, 2018), an Elgin Awards second-place winner, voted on by the international membership of the Science Fiction and Fantasy Poetry Association. She was selected by Marilyn Nelson as winner of Poetry by the Sea's inaugural sonnet competition, and then she was chosen by Julie Kane as winner of Poetry by the Sea's 2020 sonnet crown competition. Her poems appear in *AGNI, Denver Quarterly, Los Angeles Review, Massachusetts Review, Michigan Quarterly Review, Pleiades, Poet Lore, Verse Daily,* and *West Branch*. She has a B.A. in math and an M.D. and lives and works as a physician in New York City.

Dan Lonsdale is a creative writer and public school teacher. He has recently been published in *Atomic No. 26* and West Chester University's literary magazine *Daedalus*. He lives in Chester County, Pennsylvania, with his soon-to-be wife, Brooke.

Gillian Lynn Katz was born in South Africa and immigrated to the United States as a teenager in the 1960s. She grew up in the apartheid era and has written and published extensively on this subject. She recently published her poetry book *Portrait* with Kelsay Books. She also published a chapbook, *Kaleidoscope* with Finishing Line Press. She won second place in the Greenburgh Poetry Contest in 2012 and has been published in *Inkwell, Westchester Review, Epiphany, Italics Mine,* and other journals and in anthologies: *Magnum Opus 2019, Austin International Poetry Festival 2017, Best Emerging Poets 2017, Across the Long Bridge 2006*. She has a Master of Arts in Writing from Manhattanville College and a Bachelor of Arts in Literature from Purchase College. She has taught creative writing and poetry to teenagers at the Scarsdale JCC in their Summer Arts Writing Program. Ms. Katz is currently working on a novel about her experience of culture shock in combining American and South African culture into her psyche as a teenager.

Bruce McBirney lives in La Crescenta, California, where he and his wife Joanne share the good fortune to have reached senior citizen status together in one piece. They also share a hearty dismay their generation isn't leaving the world so lustrous as once hoped but wish their kids' generation the grace and insight to keep moving us forward to better things. Bruce's poems have appeared in *Rattle, America* (2002 Foley Poetry Award), *Measure, The Lyric* (2002

Roberts Memorial Prize), *The Formalist* = and other journals, and in William Baer's anthology, *Sonnets: 150 Contemporary Sonnets.*

Richard Minot is a freelance writer living in the south part of Philadelphia. He enjoys all types of poetry but is bent towards the "beat poets" such as Ferlinghetti, Ginsberg and Corso. Most of his poetry is written in this style. He has been tutoring composition at Community College of Philadelphia for many years and is a current Graduate Student at West Chester University.

Sally Nacker (MFA, Fairfield University) was a recipient of the Connecticut Audubon Society's Edwin Way Teale Writer-in-Residence at Trail Wood award in the summer of 2020. Her poem "Saying Goodbye" was inspired there. Her poem "My Father's Eighty-Fifth Birthday" originally appeared in *The Wayfarer.* She has published in numerous journals, most recently *One Art, Hawk and Whippoorwill, The Orchards Poetry Journal, The Sunlight Press, Hoot, Blue Unicorn,* and *Mezzo Cammin.* Her two collections—*Vireo* (2015) and *Night Snow* (2017)—were published by Kelsay books. Her third collection, *Kindness in Winter,* is due out in April 2021 (also by Kelsay Books). She gives thanks to Kim Bridgford.

Chris O'Carroll is the author of *The Joke's on Me* (White Violet Press, 2019). He has been a *Light* magazine featured poet, and his work has appeared in such print and online journals as *Lighten Up Online, Literary Review, Measure, The Rotary Dial,* and *The Spectator;* in several volumes of the *Potcake* Chapbooks series; and in *New York City Haiku, The Best of the Barefoot Muse, Poems for a Liminal Age, and The Great American Wise Ass Poetry Anthology.*

Kyle Potvin's chapbook, *Sound Travels on Water,* won the Jean Pedrick Chapbook Award. She is a two-time finalist for the Howard Nemerov Sonnet Award. Her poems have appeared in *Bellevue Literary Review, Whale Road Review, Tar River Poetry, Ecotone, The New York Times,* and others. Her poetry collection, *Loosen,* is available from Hobblebush Books (January 2021). Kyle lives in southern New Hampshire.

Paula Puchala Timpson writes poetry daily for Gods glory. Her thirteen-year-old son, Jimmy, is her forever Muse. Paula writes freelance articles for children's, parent's, and women's magazines, and her self-published poetry and children's books may be found on Amazon.

Anna Schostak was born and raised in West Chester and furthered her education at West Chester University, where she graduated in the spring of 2020 with a degree in English Writing and a minor in Media and Culture. It was there Anna unveiled her love for writing poetry, specifically sonnets. In addition to her passion for writing, she is also an aspiring florist. Anna uses writing and floral design to express her creativity for God's glory.

Leslie Schultz (Northfield, Minnesota) has published three collections of poetry, *Still Life with Poppies: Elegies, Cloud Song*, and C*oncertina* (Kelsay Books, 2016, 2018, 2019), and a chapbook, *Living Room*, (MWPH). Her poetry has appeared in *Able Muse, Blue Unicorn, Mezzo Cammin, MockingHeart Review, Naugatuck River Review, North Dakota Quarterly, Poet Lore, Third Wednesday, The Midwest Quarterly, The Orchards,* and *The Wayfarer*, and in the sidewalks of Northfield. She has three times had winning poems the Maria W. Faust sonnet contest (2013, 2016, 2019) and has once been nominated for a Pushcart Prize (2017). One of her haiku was included on the most recent MAVIN mission to Mars. Schultz posts poems, photographs, and essays on her website: www.winonamedia.net. She will be forever grateful for the example set by Kim Bridgford, for her beautiful, steely poems, as well as her steadfast encouragement.

Pat Valdata is a fiction writer and poet. Her new novel, *Eve's Daughters,* was published by Moonshine Cove in November 2020. Her other novels are *Crosswind* and *The Other Sister,* which won a gold medal from the Árpád Academy of the Hungarian Association.

Her poetry book about women aviation pioneers, *Where No Man Can Touch,* won the 2015 Donald Justice Poetry Prize. Her other poetry titles are *Inherent Vice* and *Looking for Bivalve*. A native of New Jersey, Pat lives in Crisfield, Maryland, with her husband Bob Schreiber.

Joyce Wilson has taught English at Suffolk University and Boston University. She is creator and editor of *The Poetry Porch* (www.poetryporch.com), which has been online since 1997. Her poems have appeared in many literary journals, among them *Alabama Literary Review, Poetry Ireland,* and *Salzburg Poetry Review*. Three of the poems included in this anthology are from her *chapbook, The Springhouse,* which appeared in 2010. Her chapbook *The Need for a Bridge* and a second full-length collection, *Take and Receive,* were published in May 2019.

www.ingramcontent.com/pod-product-compliance
Lightning Source LLC
Chambersburg PA
CBHW071355090426
42738CB00012B/3125